SOMETIMES A
GREAT NOTION

BOOKS BY DAVID DONNELL

SOMETIMES A
GREAT NOTION

poems

David Donnell

M&S

National Library of Canada Cataloguing in Publication

Donnell, David, 1939-
Sometimes a great notion : poems / David Donnell.

ISBN 0-7710-2826-1

I. Title.

PS8557.O54S64 2004   C811'.54   C2003-907374-2

We acknowledge the financial support of the Government of Canada through the Book Publishing Industry Development Program and that of the Government of Ontario through the Ontario Media Development Corporation's Ontario Book Initiative. We further acknowledge the support of the Canada Council for the Arts and the Ontario Arts Council for our publishing program.

Typeset in Minion by M&S, Toronto
Printed and bound in Canada

This book is printed on acid-free paper that is 100% recycled, ancient-forest friendly (100% post-consumer recycled).

McClelland & Stewart Ltd.
The Canadian Publishers
481 University Avenue
Toronto, Ontario
M5G 2E9
www.mcclelland.com

1 2 3 4 5   08 07 06 05 04

I've always wanted to dedicate a book to Ellen Seligman and now seems like an excellent time. This is a span of about 5 books from *Settlements* to the present. She has a very good eye for detail. In this particular case, she came up with the cover photo. It's a stunner.

TABLE OF CONTENTS

I

I

       I am
because I think I am.
I want you because I want you.
Descartes liked geometry because it makes sense.
Coco Chanel invented the floppy hat.
Mozart liked fresh duck eggs for breakfast.
Jürgen Habermas's *The Philosophical Discourse
of Modernity* sprawls across
my naked thigh wet from the shower
like a fold-out newspaper collage.

So here I am
                    with some green onions,
2 freshly cooked crabs
& 4 or 5 eggs. There are 3 of us tonight it is dark outside a
sort of soft milky
dark
as if some of the fat green trees are going to disappear. We are

talking about *Butch Cassidy & the Sundance Kid*,
                                        what a good film
it was – way back,
                    in the dark, I guess, way back in the dark,

Frank seems baffled. We eat the crab omelette w/ some fresh baguette
& sweet butter. Karen is sitting
with one foot up on the table
& the skirt of her loose dress folded between her thighs. It's
hot
outside & dark & even the trees are dark. It's easy to make
dinner for 3 people
for less than $10.00. Green onions, fresh

green onions, sitting on a white plate before dinner
still splashed with cool water,

a lot depends on 65¢ worth of fresh green onions.

Dark Side of the Moon was one of Pink Floyd's

2 biggest selling albums, years ago when we were innocent but we
weren't sheep etc.
We were Devo
& we were beautiful.
I think of it
tonight while I'm walking around the kitchen
making a huge avocado & bacon salad. 2 Hydro workers

are working outside in the dark rain repairing a broken
transformer. Mega City has power failures. I can see them
as clearly as colour television
but I haven't got the vaguest idea of what's wrong
with the transformer.

The days have been going by like wild horses,
& I'm a little confused.
I take off the Neil Young tape
& put on *Hejira* by Joni Mitchell. You can see

how cool I'm being – at home on a Friday evening
with Kirsten showering in the bathroom – this is heady
stuff but it's not too emotionally involving. I'm trying
to deal with
my life on a fairly rational level – I'm not
in the right mood tonight to get into Smashing Pumpkins.

One of the Hydro workers is above the transformer now
& his friend is on a standing platform of the extended yellow
crane hoist
with the large Hydro equipment truck parked below.   Is this

the dark side of the moon laid out in front of me
like a bright photograph from *Scientific American*? First
the darkness. Then this bright technicolor patch of industry
a term for What we have made? Take away this huge avocado
& bacon salad & I am helpless. What are we always trying
to forget? Darkness. What wakes us up in the morning?

Light. Like the bright light of Kirsten's yellow raincoat
coming home from her night job at 7:45 in the
morning saying, You wouldn't believe this some stupid
asshole tried to rape me on the subway.

A large colour magazine tear sheet of Winona Ryder wearing
bright red lipstick. A tape of the Chicago Art Ensemble, or a tape
of James
MacMillan, a tape of Bill Evans, a tape of John Coltrane's *Giant Steps* –
An Italian cookbook devoted to seafood recipes
for shrimps, calamari, octopus stew with new potatoes; a subscription
to *The New Yorker*.

When you walk into the Liberty
one of the waitresses gives you a big hug & finds you a table
where you can sit & order the Cab Sauvignon
which costs about 16 or 17 a bottle
                                    & you can relax
with your elbows on the table & lower your head
into a pool of interesting tidbits of gossip –
a story about a new arts group, a juicy bit about a
well-known columnist who has left for Mexico. And
you can tell *your* stories – go ahead
it's all here like a chic Kingdom Hall. But
I think I usually like the bar scene itself
better than the specific stories.
                           The clear dark
light & the voices rising & falling & the smells
of Japanese chicken & cinnamon & Thai noodles
are pleasantly interrupted by a variety
of interesting faces, a girl with wonderful breasts,
a fey young kid he looks suburban apparently has
something to do with money & he looks hot
he keeps snapping his galluses wide yellow ones.
Everyone has a different kind of sugar
or coke. I don't
need anything more than this to get back up.

> Beethoven doesn't emphasize pain in the first
Sonata
still friendly with Haydn & going out for Löwenbräu
& sausages,
> but doing something completely different, bluer,

pensive to begin with,
as if to say, What is there to do at this point in history
except rethink the entire question.
> I find myself torn
between the slow exploration
of time
in the 9th Sonata
> & the manic control of going over the top
that happens when I check out
Queens of the Stone Age at Lee's on August 14.
> It's all LH
in coordination
with right brain logic. I guess. And what am I doing

with my great life
besides writing, of course, & collecting some cheques?

I'm flopping like a fish out of water beside one ocean of music
after another, let's face it, it's a flood.

When I look into the great paintings of Kuniyoshi
from that post-Hokusai period of 1850 – 1885   new colours

since the brilliant Floating World period of the late 17th cent.
new colours
& enormous intimacies

I am amazed that western painters like Manet & Renoir
created much of a stir at all in Paris. They seem so flat

& bourgeois in comparison to the Japanese work, beautiful,
for sure
& full of a strange & almost liquid vitality

but they merely state the beautiful. We never get to see the girl
in Manet's
Girl with a Red Hat
flaunt her female exuberance

& of course Paris critics would have gone wild if someone had
taken down *Olympia*
which doesn't really look like a woman at all,

& put up that wonderful *shunga* painting of eleven men with huge
hard-ons
big red glans penis heads

all running toward each other in a wild concentric circle.

"No," she says, sitting up, "no,
I have never eaten corn bread w/ sweet butter & black bean soup
for breakfast. It sounds
                                great." So we lie in bed all day
& drink tea & read back copies of *The New Yorker*. Corn bread
& chicken soup for supper;
                                guess we'll have an egg
& some cereal for breakfast.

I like *The Kingfishers* partly because I love the bird,

           common
also in western Ontario. But you can look through most of Olson's
poems
   & you won't find a clear description of himself (he
was an impressive-looking man & a good agitator), or one of
his friends, or of a black child with an amazing face
modelling a Gap jean jacket in *Vanity Fair*.

Frank Gehry calls his new woven laminated maple strip chairs
after various hockey terms – Hat Trick, Power Play. It's okay,
I think it works.
Some of Feiffer's cartoons are better than most of Duncan's poems,
or Olson's *Maximus*.
I like some of his pamphlets, & I like his occasional use of
numbers.

Although Gloucester is a beautiful idea. A place
where
convention
doesn't pile up & become confusing.

The grackles come out in the early morning & the fishermen
come in before lunch. And those are Atlantic fish, no
freshwater grub.
      I miss description in Olson
– I miss classic outline
         & significant detail. But

I like *The Kingfishers*. He builds
a coherent & extrapolative world around his
indigenous
          image. Alludes to some events
in his life
        & has room left
in the poem for a sense
of their strange & almost comic funkiness.

I have given up worrying about MIR. Every time
the Russian cosmonaut fixes one wiring panel Michael Foale blows
the connection he was trying for on the central computer
in a different part of the station. This is high-tech adventure.
I think of them moving outside into the milky darkness of outer space
floating along their lifelines
in cumbersome spacesuits
& I don't know whether to take it seriously or not. I think MIR
is a shared bid for world domination.
"How long did it take you to arrive at that, you chump?" says my
friend Jack, we're at the bar, & we're killing time.
I say, I don't know, I think I was initially struck by the whole
poetic, technological image of the shuttle flights, it was colourful,
it made me think of Alcibiades, of Plato, of the Trojan Wars.
The newspapers talk about energy & space exploration & mining.
This makes me laugh. Mining? Can you imagine newsboys
walking up & down Yonge Street selling copies of the *Northern Miner*
& the *Financial Times* & calling out Extra, Extra, Big Mine Deposits
Discovered on Mars.
                    Of course, I still like my initial image. I'm
an Optimist, I guess. But they've been up there too long
without discovering something like a Space Kangaroo or Martian oranges,
& the radio announcers always screw up the technical wording
of their news capsules, & then move on to Israel or war-torn Lebanon

or Egypt or the Congo. O yes, O yes, by the waters of Babylon
I sat down & wept.

    Because there was nothing else for me to do. Like Alcibiades
    some time after the Trojan Wars, weeping after the death of his best
friend, or perhaps because I'm a stupid bastard, & I'm unemployed,
    & I'd like to be out there myself. For Christ's sake, Don't shoot,
    I'm unarmed, & I'm in my goddamn shirt sleeves.

> They had never seen such a storm. It
>
>   lasted
>
> for 40 days or 50 days. Then
> it was over. A few months later
>
> in Arabic & Hebrew & Persian
> there were 17 new words for darkness.

ALEX COLVILLE

        I like Alex Colville's paintings. They're a sort of
autobiography
                of his life at a northern latitude jutting out
into the Atlantic seaboard,
                        Wolfville, N.S., to be precise.
not that far north of New York.
                        But I have problems
with a lot of people. "Is Colville," they say,
"a great painter like Titian or Velasquez?" And I say, No, he's not a
great
painter. Like Titian or Velasquez. And they say, "O well, is he

an experimental painter?" I guess they think it's logical
if you can't be a great painter then, presto, you paint stripes
on a dark blue background & naturally you call it
                                "Stripes."
Anyway, I say, No, he's not an experimental
painter. And they say, "O too bad."

What we do get is wonderful eastern seaboard
paintings of nude sunbather & crows, or a man on a bicycle
& a crow flying past, or the dark horse charging the oncoming
locomotive at night

that Bruce Cockburn used as the cover for one of his albums,
or the naked couple beatific in front of
the open refrigerator at night. It
                        doesn't look like New York
& it doesn't look like Venice in the 1560s; okay, that's cool,

it looks like here & now & it's just a tad commercial,
maybe, but that's okay too. He paints us the way we are. No,
I don't think he's a great painter. I just think he's terrific –
enjoyable, informative, & I can look at his paintings
for a long time without blinking.

Bill Johnson
who came up to Ontario feckless from
Washington State to study with Étienne Gilson   quoted Sartre
to me one evening down in the laundry room of the old
Trinity Apartments building on Harbord Street. Aloneness, I think,
was the subject. I think he paraphrased, "The Lonely flee to
Aloneness."
But I've wondered since, I wonder if Jean-Paul Sartre
really knew anything about Aloneness at all. Maybe he was
just a bright sociable guy who wrote 4 or 5 extraordinarily clear books
& became famous & was written up in *Time.*

And then I thought of Bill's face –

blond, rugged, boyish, very enthusiastic,
that first semester when he came up here.

Did he wind up teaching somewhere in Seattle?
Did he ever marry that lovely girl he was engaged to
the 60-minute marathon telephone conversations they used to have
long distance

she who had been in a convent
for 2 years before they met on campus?

Quite a few years have passed
I haven't had a conversation

like that since,

                      but I've lost a few socks,
I met Laura in a blast of hot steam
& I think I've had a towel
stolen at least once.

Now the whole world is falling on Wynton's head
because
of his walking across the street to play Handel. His SPY desk calendar,
2 new suits,
& yellow Mercedes Benz
are all falling on his head. "Beans," she says, "look at it

this way. We are as good as it gets." The red towel,
the familiar worn hardwood kitchen door sill,
a discussion of various non-depictive schools of art after rehearsal
downtown at the Oasis bar & grill. This is as good

as it gets. "Hokay," I say. Wet from the shower, I have no
reason to argue
do I? A simple piece of flounder for supper,
tan grill marks from the wire grill under the broiler,
& asparagus in a quick butter sauce.
                                             It's not good to eat
too much after being in the studio all day. The piece of flounder
has the same shape as Hudson County in west Tennessee. W
                                             doesn't
come from west Tennessee & neither do I
but the idea of putting Handel on the same tapes with a Charlie
Mingus composition & 2 Nina Simone songs
is a good/idea.

      I had never done it before
                    but
obviously it doesn't take a ton of expertise.
It was at a friend's house
                not at *Sam's*
in Albany or summer employment at a hotel in Nova Scotia
one of those places with white linen
& they bring you the melted butter in a silver pot.
                                        It's
easy. You need a good knife. Short blade
w/ a wide centre
& a thick wooden handle. Skroom
click grate scrape wiggle
                snap.
$9.85 worth of fresh Atlantic oysters are yours.
The dark grey top ½ of the shell pops up flush
suspended by its hinge
that delicate tie of grey material broken. And
there it is
                pale light
glistening sensitive pearly bivalve.
The shell looks at least 2,000 years old,
but the bivalve is extraordinarily fresh
& brand new. I don't know if it quivers. I eat it with a sop
of lemon juice,
                    a daub of red sauce
& gaze at the profoundly empty shell. Bermuda; Pistol Bay, N.S. There
are millions of oysters in the world & they're all pale
& they all taste of the ocean.

       Death comes on little
tiny
feet
     like the slow smoky burnt fog from the rust & rotting
undersides
of moored ships in the greater Chicago harbour
that Carl Sandburg describes
so beautifully simply as the early morning fog

coming in unexpectedly as the light changes
after a clear night

when death came for Laura Nyro it came in the form of a
Heroin overdose & she didn't know what happened

John Coltrane – who was perhaps the Great Poet of the 1960s –
death came
in the form of a Heroin overdose & he didn't know what happened

Richard Fariña – who wrote *A Long Time Coming & A Long Time Gone* –
knew what happened for a few minutes perhaps
a 26-storey building turned upside down
& the sky turned a bright orange
                         as he was thrown from his
motorcycle en route to the launch of his first book.

But Death & all his dominions came very slowly
for Mr. William S.
                    Burroughs. Someone asked him at a party once
"Where do you think we go after we die?" And Burroughs said,

"How the hell do you know you're not dead now?" Paranoids live
for
a long time. It took a lot of slow moves from the harbour
to get close
to the heels of those St. Louis dancing shoes.

OLD MASTERS

Those dark
          old masters
of the 20th century Henry Miller whose friends called him

Hank
or sometimes Hen
               & William S for Seward
– named after Lincoln's Secretary of State
who bought Alaska from the Russians for a cheap 75 million –
Burroughs

will we still read them
will we still bleed them   now that it's 2002? Well,

I don't know,
          we still read Herodotus & Aristophanes,

don't we?

      Am I going out of my fucking mind? That scene Bill
SYKES,
      & Nancy, O, & the dog, the little DOG,   on the ROOF, a slate roof,
this is obviously AFTER the poorhouse,
BUT,
      HOW does Dickens bring these people into his narrative of *Oliver Twist*?

      I can't beleeeeve it – of course, I'm very innocent,   inno cente   BUT
the Republicans
                    are going after Bill Clinton AGAIN   – claiming SIC   that
      they
have NEW material on the Monica Lewinsky affair.

I don't know why W.B. Yeats was so intoxicated
about Byzantium
or why he would write such lines as, "Once out
of nature, I shall never take . . . ," etc.
I had everything lined up   & then I
blew it.
People under 19 have a fabulous capacity for hanging out & doing
nothing but I don't seem
to have that ability any more.
I guess Yeats was tired
of bloody Dublin & more than a little tired of 2 or 3
women
none of whom shall be mentioned here. But
it's a lovely poem.

LEMON PIE

      little lemon meringue pie clouds
sequenced like notes
on a pale clear blue sky 6:55 a.m.
yes it's very pretty, Mr. Weather God;
Schopenhauer would say, O,
das ist eine common illusion,
common, the world is a picture-postcard,
that's Schopenhauer's *The World as Will and Idea*.
But what did Schopenhauer know about
astrophysics?

       All these neat little boîte cafés
Lost Camel with its fab 6 × 4
wooden overhead sign on Queen
St. W. for example, bakery cafés
everything in Toronto is blank
cum blank.com these days.
The provimi veal at Le Paradis
a bistro not a boîte is upscale,
or you can go for Turkish & get baba ga
nosh so good you drool at a little place
on Elm St. with 2 tables & chairs.
My pick these days – the spanakopita at
Acropolis Bakery & Café east of Pape.
You can drink 2 great coffees on top
of it & feel like heaven.

COCOA

Cocoa, dish soap, lemon yellow
splash in a white saucer
sitting over by the windowsill.
I don't have any gods this morning.
I lost the Tropic of Capricorn yesterday.
There it was, on my globe, Australia & Johannesburg & South
Uruguay.
                    Clear as a photo one minute & then I lost it.
Happiness is impossible.
You don't have to be angry, Harry, you don't have to do anything.
She looks so innocent *innocente* in that yellow sundress
you can think of nothing except slipping
those pale green panties down with one thumb
& discovering beauty bare.
Good-bye Euclid, what did you know about anything?

I don't have any gods this morning but half an hour ago
I discovered the Horse latitudes &
this is what I look like coming out of the shower naked.

I eat the last of the strawberries
after you left
                    sitting with my feet up on the white pine rail
in the ½ dark of the back deck. The red lamp flutters
a bit it's late & there are 2 or 3
large moths hanging around the way moths do.
This is almost a scene from the 17th century in the south of Japan.

Thinking of the sweetness of your mouth
kissing you with the strawberries still there
of how blue your eyes are
under the red hair pulled back with a black band
darkness of your nipples
flatness of your long stomach how it ripples
down to the band of your pants.
                              Sitting here with my bare feet
up on the white pine & a large bulge in my dark green People's
Republic of China work pants. The deck is cool with some breeze
rustling through the big oak tree
                              & that odd not quite ¾ moon
don't know how I would describe it – not yellow, like edam,
not tawny, a mid-June ¾ moon,
                              lazy night, your sweetness
but no indigo girls dancing at the blue centre. There are so
many parts of the body, toes, earlobes, buttocks, shoulder blades,
too many to count. Sure, I'm looking forward to seeing you for supper
on Saturday.

And as for me,
I'm obviously uptight this morning, the bulldog's been chewing
at my summer house sandals,
                    my left hip is killing me
& Jennifer my beautiful therapist doesn't have any perfect solution.

There is no perfect solution to a life of Gertrude Stein,
even
Picasso didn't know that she loved brie cheese.

I look physically fit. I should
I do a lot of exercises.

I've been working a lot, I have
published books in a variety of stores,

I'm still concentrating on all the big abstract questions,
is Hans Hofmann still significant,
what is life without Simone de Beauvoir,
you know, all that sort of stuff,
is there life out there in TV Iowa?

When O when will I discover the logic of the multifidus
& after that What ever happened to that chartered accountant
I used to know in the 70s who smoked the best red dirt Mexican rough cut
I've ever tasted.
                    Jesus, that was good stuff.

O LUST, I SUPPOSE & BITTER LEMONS

      I thought of your thighs last night
I was in the shower looking at my own thighs
that shower brush from Noah's dripping with suds
how the mind photographs things
you were in the background or grounded by light
the shower water was hot & I saw everything
very clearly O I can see the beauty of your little
finger the pinky O so clearly now
there was olive oil on the fullness of your thighs
sweet to the taste & crumbs of spanakopita

your animal honked at me I could see her very clearly
most beautiful of all things most beautiful of
all natural plants; O how I want you, how I want
your thighs on my shoulders & let me lick each of
those crumbs of spanakopita.
                  The ouzo will come later
sitting with my arm around your shoulders
& then after desire has been sated after you
have tired of me – after I am a castoff rowboat –
there will be bitter lemons
fresh from the sink with drops of
cool water on them. Then
I will praise the lemons
their freshness I will praise everything yellow.

      The Japanese monks of the late 19th
century
         spent quite a lot of time
on the question of Noh-Mind,
                    by which they meant –
an open ness & emptiness at once,

a large bowl of pure green tea
listening to itself hum. And after the mind

has listened to itself for about ½ an hour
then it begins naturally tuning
to other parts of the body

the toes speak   the left hip has something to say

the buttocks speak   the genitals speak

the big red pear of the heart speaks
& the muscles in the right shoulder sing a little ditty

all the parts of the body say, Why are we here
is there any fresh pink lamb for supper
what is there in life besides swimming & walks
& thinking?

STEPHEN HAWKING & LIGHT

                    Around late June somebody up in heaven
must spill a tub of soft butter into the air.
                                        Partly
the heat perhaps, & the way light bounces off so much
foliage & bright glass;
                            but this light which lasts into
late August, this light,
                            goddammit, this particular
Summer Light
                    makes the entire
city as clear as an endless astronomical circuit –
every ash, elm, maple,
                    every child dropping a strawberry
popsicle on the pavement & crying, "O poopsy,"
every Samantha slipping
into a loose summer dress & feeling that she's the most
beautiful girl in town,
                            even ideas, lost emotions, stray ends,
all become clear.
                    That's what you want
isn't it, Stephen Hawking. Clear?

I fell in love with Luce on a blue day
over a conversation about artichokes & lemons.
It's her face that captivates me   its essential radiance
when she smiles
not her gorgeous body.
She does wonderful things with summer dresses.
But it's her face that captivates me   it's essential radiance
that close-cut dark curly hair
those almandine eyes
I always thought almonds were white & come in chocolate cake
but hers are dark dark brown with a very faint slant to them.
It's her face that brings my Oscar Homolka panting to the edge
    of my pants
like a dachshund puppy at the edge of a blue lake.
It's that Roman nose even though she's Lebanese
it's that mouth
that elegiac smile or is it elegiac is it thoughtful pensive I guess
not her left breast tumbling out of a dark blue cardigan
that first night kissing goodbye at her doorway.

I love her in bluejeans & I love her in a sexy off-the-shoulder dress
it's her face that captivates me
& the first sentence that comes out of her mouth is always hello.

BARTENDER

She was all mouth & long legs
& I fell in love with her instantly as she came out from
the bar area to pick up some glasses.

Proust was a master of sadness,
that is,
he accepted the fact of his own resignation
almost as a fact of history,
a subordinate region in the great land of the world,
he doesn't struggle

acceptance is the large word here
accept the loss of childhood accept

a flirtatious memory of adolescence.
But he turns deeply   into the heart   of his
own narrative. Accept your take
on Swann & the Princess de Guermantes
& accept them both as language signs

moving continually away from the young Proust,

melancholy, a little drunk,
he pulls them back like amazing kites.

Arendt had other things
to do. Essays to write, black coffee
w/ brown sugar at 2 o'clock in the morning.
She liked Mahler but he
                         wasn't her favourite composer.
The photographs of her as a young
                              student when she first met MH
seem to be of a girl who is lost.
The photographs of her at a later age
show a woman who seems to have
been enriched by all she has been torn apart by
or is that a contradiction.
                     At any rate
she didn't come to America
just for the glory of the sun falling on Prospect Park
or despite the occasional young man like Philip Rahv,
handsome moody talented totally sincere,

                         just to get involved in some scenes
                         with *Partisan Review*.

The problem with catching up
to the past if you weren't
there in the first place

is that you have to read other people who
are usually sorters of stories. Edmund
Wilson for example, or people in *The New Yorker*.
Hannah Arendt didn't actually dis-
like Mary McCarthy & she Arendt
certainly wasn't in league with
Lillian Hellman – she thought
Hellman was flighty, may have
seen her one famous play & probably never got around to reading
Pentimento.

In the Grade 13 boys' Locker Room. There isn't a single boy
here who isn't secretly thrilled by the size of his cock.
But the general air of behaviour is pandemonium & banter & gym socks
tossed at the head of another boy who is bending over to get his Adidas
out from under Brad's eqpt. bag where they have become misplaced.
Wow, someone says to Brian in the showers, are you huge,
what do you know or do at night. And everybody howls with laughter.
Brian is being centred out as The Wanker. Nothing; he says,
you're crazy, I don't do anything at all, it's genetic.
Or if Paul says the same thing to Harry, Harry just puts his hands
arms crossed up on his shoulders & closes his eyes under the shower jet
& shakes his head. He says, I don't even think about things like
that.

"America is just too large," she says,
we are
standing on the Williamsburg Bridge,

we are in love at this moment & she is wearing a loose
orange knit jersey dress with bare shoulders
& running shoes

I am leaning on my elbows looking down at the muddy
water
& I am thinking
about Chas. Ives & how he changed American music forever
& about Raymond Chandler's novels
& about Maria Muldaur singing "Midnight at the Oasis"

& she is gesturing at what I'm not completely sure.

I'm ecstatic at this moment & I want to fly to California
for a few days. She's restless,
charismatic
& has beautiful ankles.

Her father was in the restaurant equipment business
in Chicago. She is never happy.

One of my friends when I was about 20 said, I like girls who fall into my hands like a ripe peach. He didn't say peaches, there was no es. He may possibly have been thinking about one girl in particular, as do we all, shaving in the mornings, I'm sure, or getting dressed to go out for dinner. O yes, Frank, now, at a somewhat later age, I commend you, I call you to the front of the class to raise your hands & speak simply & from the heart.

All this Berkeley talk about contingency / a tall
shaggy angel – hands in his pockets – trying to sit on a butterfly pin;

Is this where Naboakov – his pronunciation – came up with his novel *Pnin*?

CARPENTER'S HANDS

She likes the feel of his carpenter's hands on her
breasts, wide, tapered, not blunt-fingered,
they are just rough enough to be interesting.

This is the way Clara tells it. She says, Now David's got everything
figured out. W.G. Sebald is THE new author of the moment. We're in bed,
& I'm sitting up with my back against the wall naked reading *Vertigo*,
that's the book David thinks is really great, about 20 minutes at a time,
out loud. And then he'll say to me, Aren't you enjoying this a lot,
reading it out loud, your voice is wonderful. And I say, O yeah, it's great,
& then the next thing I know he's got my foot in his mouth.

Watching Liz examine the melon we're eating
with intense interest in how she might describe the exact shade of green
between melon & rind.
"It's so green," she keeps saying, her eyes enraptured,
her mouth gorgeous,
"It's so ripe & it's so green."

At night, after the 4–12 shift
– this is an industrial bakery called Weston's
where they have huge tubs on the floor that go maybe 12 feet
in dia
meter, not the sort of corner bakery you find in an Italian
neighbourhood where you walk in & get ½ a doz. Calabrese rolls
& ½ a lb. of Genoa salami –
                         a tall figure in white pants
rolled up at the cuff & a white smock appears
& rolls out a big cylindrical drum of yeast
for the next shift. Frank,
                    that's his name, simple,
tall & slim as a basketball player, reflective, long dark pony
tail down ½ way to his waist,
                         & his friend Raoul, a Haitian guy
who came to Toronto from Montreal sometime last year,
shorter than Frank's 6'3" & stocky & very cheerful,
not as melancholy as Frank/but also very into music

anyway,
         Lord, these 2 guys,
come downtown looking for a late spot to have a drink
for coffee, for action,
                    for colourful talk,
maybe Queen Street West some little bar or bar salon
or a drive east out by the Beaches
                              but some place
where they may have a little food in the kitchen
& sometimes
              on certain nights, they have music. Good.

DID KEITH JARRETT EVER RECORD
"WHAT ARE YOU DOING FOR THE REST OF YOUR LIFE?"

        The Skinhead & his girlfriend who wears 2
pairs of leggings are shopping for vegetables.
I have no idea what this means do they put soy & mustard
on their fingers & lick it off like cats   at least broccoli
tastes but you have to let the soy soak into it
while it's steaming in a pool of juice beside the brown
rice.   Clinton says over & over that we have to discover
customers in Mexico
                        Mexico, Jesus,
in order
            to get back
the money that has been displaced because big companies
like Sansui
                so who owns Sansui   I own a 4-channel Pioneer
have been shipping enormous contracts out of America
& giving it to Mexican workers
who do it for 8 dollars a day.   Why do I have to be
involved in these questions? Obviously
the northern bourgeoisie are shifting their assets. I have a B.A.
but my best job so far was a warehouse clerk. Now I'm unemployed
for the winter. A huge series of chemical tank cars
blew up in Mississauga last night. We were asleep. Sandy's
black silk stockings tossed casually over the back of a straight
backed maple chair. One of our few pieces of furniture   we have
cushions

on the floor   a classic frying pan, & the new Keith Jarrett
tape
        At the Deer Head Inn recorded live at his old bar in the Pocono
mountains
in Pennsylvania. Clear sound. There is no loose money
floating around. The big companies take care of themselves
like big cats. The Skinhead & his girlfriend are shopping for
vegetables.
There is probably no loose money floating around in Pennsylvania
either.
I have a package of frozen fish sticks & 4 tins of Heinz
spaghetti. I have no idea why she wears
2 pairs of leggings & she has a large ring in her left nostril.
                                                        There are

no jobs, the streets are full of garbage
it's hot & drivers speed up at the last second before the light.

50

MARTIANS

       you see me as a goodlooking whiteguy
but this is el disagreement temps perdu

because I see myself as a really hot performer
with large hands
& a rather unusual long face – a superior person,

a high IQ

a martian with pale skin
& straw-
coloured hair w/ a punk haircut.

First they overwork you until you start drinking
too much scotch; then they break your heart; then they take you out in a field
& shoot you.

We were talking about the Floating World
& I said
to my friend Luke,
What I really want is to relate
or connect or hook up
my chaotic subjectivity
with a large stable major theory of the Big Picture.

And Luke said to me, Ha, ha. That's not orthodox Buddhism. Orthodox
Buddhism
says that the world IS a floating world –

regardless of your fascinating & subjective persona.

O Hell, I said,
Can't I be myself

& do Zen
& think about history
you know all at the same time?

Ha, ha,
says Luke.
no, not you, Pal. Just drink your coffee & be glad
you're alive.
And I say, I am glad I'm alive
my right arm is torn off at the shoulder
but I'm still talking.

AT THE ONLY BAR

        I'm at The Only Bar
& it's night
& everybody's drinking & laughing.

I'm probably the only person here who is just a tad melancholy.

She has a black nothing dress on
& if she bought it herself
she probably paid about 500.

Amazing how some of those design shops down
on Queen & up on St. Clair & out on the Danforth,
Sarah's for example,
or that cute place Risque on Bloor West,
can put a dress together that promises
& suggests everything you can imagine.

She says I've had men do lots of outrageous things,
one man paid me to have sex while he watched.

I say What do you do now, you're gorgeous,
& she smiles & says Well I'm not a stockbroker
uh, I'm a fulltime dancer.

I'm turned on.
I say Can I tell you something really intimate?
Sure she says & she moves all of her gorgeous self right up against me.
I say What I really want is to wash your hair & have sex
at the same time. Oh she says I've had lots of promises like that,

Like that song by Leonard Cohen, *Take This Waltz*,
she rolls her blue eyes,
let your fingers do the walking, let your imagination do the talking.
She's hipper than I am.

Well okay I say, Baudelaire had to make a living & Walt
Whitman loved the stars & you've got a living. It's dark
outside & I'm a little drunk & it's
showtime.

A lot of people are writing in geek – age 27 – ese these days,
these days
         there aren't enough burnt umber wheat fields these days

I think perhaps I'll dye my hair red & get it cut in spiky tufts.
This will be a new image.
Goodbye to my favourite big shirt & faded corduroys.
This will bring the under30s into the bookstores
to buy my books
         ha ha ha ha ha ha ha ha
They can't read but they're good on soap operas & they're good
on brand names
         Nikes suck. The Prospector original is too heavy.

"What do you think of contemporary literature in general,"
she asked me,
         she was supposed to be doing an interview.
I said, Too much obsession with personal pain
& not enough narrative surprise. Nobody's searching for the golden
fleece
      & by the end of this interview
we'll be in a bar
& you'll be saying, O wow, no, you didn't like really
listen to Red Skelton when you were 9 years old?

bet your imac.
bet your sweet ass.

II

      tap   Tap   TAp   the roundfaced blind boy
with spacedout blue eyes & a childish mouth
                              comes tapping
& slashing with his white cane
through the round tables of Dooney's outdoor patio. "The world
is going to end the world is going to end the world is going
to ENd." He stops at our table & I give him two dollars.
But I've had supper & it seems appropriate. "Loonie," he says,
rubbing his thumb across the smooth coin. He's blind,
or almost blind & he thinks it's the bullshit Ottawa one dollar
coin with a big western Ontario Loon on one side. "No, no,"
I tell him,
          "it's two dollars. TWO. It's like a loonie,
but it's silver,
             & it's got a copper circle in the middle
with a big Polar Bear on one side. It's the bullshit Ottawa
two dollar coin, & it's got a big Polar Bear on one side."
"Thanks," he says,
           rubbing his thumb over the bear,
"it's the first one I've had. I like bears." And then he moves
on,
    swinging his white cane back & forth between the tables,
"The world is going to end the world is going to end the world
is going" all over again, To END – at the patio doorway
& almost collides with young Emilio who has 2 plates on
each arm & at least one of them was calamari.

He said, I don't have a good side & a bad side. He said,
I'm like a porterhouse steak, ha ha, I'm the same on both sides.
O wow, I thought to myself, am I looking to lay a couple of big fresh eggs
sunnyside on this guy
& see where the hell this conversation about medians & eschatology
really takes us

            I guess you can tell he's Tibetan at first
glance,
          he has that squarish face, a small cap
& a large red robe   made of some fairly heavy woollen
material
                    a sort of caftan.

much different from the cassocks Catholic
priests wear,
            which is amazing.
                          It's sunny & he walks with a calm
purposeful ½ smile on his rugged face. He looks as if
he has just gotten off a plane from Tibet

& is walking along Dupont Street at lunch time with nothing
on his mind except the pleasure of a chicken salad sandwich

eaten out of the waxed paper as he walks along. "4½ million,"
one of his friends says to him who has come to meet him
in the parking lot. "4½ million," he says, nodding appreciatively,

"a big city."

40

I'm over 40 now, blue sky, cool night.
I think I've already pushed the sides of the envelope open.
Now I'm trying to advance the position of the envelope in space.
Position ambience – as in, the ambience of physics.

We are all going to die some day. I don't want to talk about that.
Some days a woman is a bright lemon yellow Saab.
Some days a woman is a woman.

John Ashbery has so many friends, where did Mr. Softsoap get them all?

I'm beautiful, I'm handsome.
I think people are often jealous of me for silly reasons.

I've written some great poems but I'm not making any money.

I have to give up my interest in girls like Reese Witherspoon
modelling a halter dress in *Details* magazine Ciba colour.
That was back in the summer, good god, I have to start being realistic.

The Future is as clear to me as Palomar – I'm going to sleep well
& devote my high C energy afternoons

to writing perfect descriptions of asparagus, the photographs
of Imogen Cunningham. the girl's face when she spilled
a ssssclurp of mustard on her white English tennis shorts.

I hope the next girlfriend is a redhead,
& I wind up diving into her bed
without breaking my leg.

SANDY TIME

LAST NIGHT I had supper around 8. And then
I was sitting in the kitchen working on some notes.
                                        And I noticed
that the clock & the calendar, both in the kitchen,
were making me feel very static.
                            I'd been annoyed
for about a week with several friends with whom I'd had a
falling out, 2 friends, a cowboy & a girl who was really a tease.

            And I began to think about time itself
rather than the falling out.
                        I don't mean clocks,
I mean Time,
that question or substantive entity
philosophers like Hawking or Jean-Paul Sartre
have debated for centuries,
                            since long before the Greeks
I suppose,
            the Greeks were not obsessed with time,
they were obsessed with timelessness,
                                but anyway, let me continue,
I decided that Time was a determined sector in the shape of
a bottle,
        let's say a quart, with a pretty formal label
of let's say Teacher's,
                    one of my favourites,
                                    & what I would do

is walk into the bottle,
                  happily,
                                not at all in a Hank Williams
kind of way,
                  & Leonard, he's never answered me when I've called him
up either, & my mother was a friend of one of his cousins.

AUGUST

August drops me out of
the hot skillet & leaves me gasping.
The next week blows my battered yacht
into a tranquil blue calm.
Apollo is the only god & Apollo is
the god of love. He watches over me
while I sleep. Last month's *Vanity Fair*
on the floor beside my bed. All those photos
of Martha Stewart kitchens arouse my libido.
Sleep calmly, he says, she loves you
& only you.
You stupid god, I tell him, get her scanties
down over her knees & PAST that delicate
white heel. Then I will believe in you
& you won't find me wasting my time
on soccer games & I will offer flowers & fresh
mangoes at your shrine.

I said,
          You look like the sort of girl
who probably knows a lot about Euclid's *Principles*

of Geometry. She was standing at the bar

looking great very slim great bones in a loose shirt
& steel rim glasses
& loose pants. I don't know. Maybe I was thinking

of that great line from Raymond Chandler, She had more
curves
than a scenic highway, I fell in love with her on first sight.

And she said,
               No, I don't know a goddamn thing
about
Euclid. She smiled. It was a great smile

sort of like a pink flower opening in the morning

& I liked that, it was so quick & honest.

So she left her friends for about half an hour
& we sat down at a table on the far side
& talked about her. She was in theatre,

she's a set designer, she's sort of apprenticing,
up & down,
                    that's life, & she invited me to a play,
When Harry Met Sally. I hope she realizes

that the title was first used by Harry Connick Jr., you know,
New Orleans, jazz, southern voices & Bourbon,
                                                                    all that stuff.
But I've got the address & I'm going to see the play.

Aloes are supposed to be bitter.
I have
no bitterness about our casual ending.
I didn't want it to happen, but it just happened.
Juicy white onion is sweet when you pick it up
from the oil & penne of the salad
& chew it slowly. Lemons are sour. Well,
I suppose they are, there's that classic joke
about the guy standing in front of the trumpet
playing sucking a half lemon
& the trumpet player can't hit a fair note
to save his life.
                    That's the way I feel about you
occasionally when we bump effortlessly
into each other at someone's house.
I'm like you know laughing & talking
& coming down the hallway
& there you are in the kitchen
standing with your legs spread wide apart in that black
skirt & some other guy is with you. Who
invited this dumb dick along for the hayride?
But you're always sweet & your hair smells
like fresh grass & somebody else came into
my life too
                & now they're being hard
to get along with. I think we were 2 of a kind

both in love & looking for someone else.

My only take on the word bitter
is when they use it in a sports commentary
after the Leafs lose 3-2,
or one of my favourite beers
Conners Best Bitter – it's got great taste
& a great body & it's made right here in Ontario.

This is Brian Mulrooney's favourite joke.
"There was a chicken,
now."
     He has the good dark blue suit on & he can't resist slapping
his thigh with pleasure at the very thought of this joke
that is almost as old as Ur.
                 He has a glass
of his favourite whisky, a rye whisky, Seagram's, what else, we
are after all fairly close to the sea, not far from the Atlantic,
& very close to New Hampshire too as far as that goes. "There
was a chicken," he says, leaning back a bit in the brown & black leather
fitted armchair & slapping one dark blue thigh, "There was a chicken
that wanted to cross the road."

Winona Ryder's on the cover of *US*
this week looking sexy & vivacious
as usual
        tank top & a dark blue hook & anchor on her shoulder
turned to the reader. She's lovely

& sometimes she shows her breasts & sometimes she doesn't.
Tempestuous young woman one minute,
                                or one film, okay,
& the next thing you know she's a celestial young
version of Audrey Hepburn
for the 1990s.

        You don't show your breasts very much.
I'm not being egregious. I just mean you wear sweaters
a lot,
        they're not loose, not tight, dark grey is a favourite
colour,
        you seem to favour blacks & greys a lot. But you show
your legs a lot.
                You've got great legs.

        Dark brown hair with 3 streaks of peroxide
almost like corn braids, & that gorgeous face
w/ the sudden changes of expression & the WIDE smile. You're so
casual you're almost like wind; you're so desirable
I can taste your mouth like apple or fresh mango.

CONFUSION'S JUST ANOTHER WORD

I confused *A Long Day's Journey into Night*
with *Death of a Salesman* this morning.
I don't know why.
I was washing my face at the basin with Ivory soap
& thinking about plays,
                              both have sons in them.
We're supposed to think mostly about adults.
I don't know, I guess adults buy theatre tickets
but the boys are more interesting.

Life in general happens in a blur.
You remember the key players that you have to remember.
Boy would Sara be upset if I called her Patti.

There are 2,876,492 words in the *OED*.
17 different species of giraffe just in Kenya. The number of
birds in America is astronomical. I read a 4 × 5 pocket guide
on snake species & I couldn't believe the diversity. They're all
snakes & most of them eat frogs if they get a chance. I sure hope
you don't forget this poem. It's so good. You will. I'll live.

POWDER

I think of that song
                          can't remember who
sings it   I've got a little powder on my nose,
& I don't care
                  a dark pretty voice with throaty
up bouncy phrasing very much like yours when you came here
from Indiana
                    & now you've latched on to a terrific rock group
& you're going to Texas sometime in the fall.

like a blue denim shirt you put on in the morning, tails,
soft collar,
                take it off at night it falls in a heap on the
polished hardwood floor.

I think of that song
                          can't remember who
sings it   I've got a little powder on my nose
& I don't care   throaty, soft, a lot like yours
when you came here from Indiana with a suitcase of sheet music
& 2 dresses.

Fans were a little ticked off with the July *Esquire*,
it was the dumb photograph
of men in asbestos suits on the cover,
something to do with firefighting. It was a bit ridiculous,

Capitalism in the magazine industry is obviously in trouble,
Details, GQ
& *Gear*
are probably going to pick up most of the *Esquire* constituency.
Gear had Jaime Pressly on the cover in August
with a beautifully designed splash of colour type –
nudity
media love
robbing gas stations

& Jaime Pressly is the most gorgeous girl in America.
Arts guys are reading magazines like *Elle* & *Vogue*.
Hetero guys are reading magazines like *Cosmo*
just to pick up on what people are talking about.
Elle says the New Look is Bold Feminine & Chic. It sounds

just like 1982, but – design & colour – they brought it off.
Cosmo has a wonderful subhead for August
set next to a gorgeous 24 year old model in a black leather bustier –
    How to squash his
        post nooky paranoia.

That's amazing & absurd, isn't it?

Guys don't get enough nooky

I think *Wired* & *Fast Company* & *Scientific American*
& *Harper's* & *The Atlantic* & even *The New Yorker* have
all these popular magazines beat by a mile. O, I forgot, somebody called
Billy Crudup turned up on the cover of *Esquire*
looking vaguely bemused in the gorgeous hot month of August.

Henry
                Miller had the opportunity
to be a great writer, but he didn't want to write brilliant
finished books like Dostoyevsky's *Crime and Punishment*
or D.H. Lawrence's *Women in Love*. Miller spoke for his own
work when he said, "Most fiction is made up in plots
about people who aren't really the characters the novelist
pretends they are, I just want to write about my life."

And so he did,
                manuscript after manuscript pile,
8 pages of mundane descriptive bullshit followed with almost
no transition by 8 pages of brilliant plunging & probing
reportage on his life, his life in America & Paris.
Too much New York & Paris at times perhaps.
                                        Flipping through
Sexus, Plexus & *Nexus,*
                        the three long books of *The Rosy*
Crucifixion, I am amazed
at the amount of
garbage he includes. But every 8 or so pages he breaks through
& introduces you to someone, creates an amazing little event
or goes off on one of his long soaring rants
about the inequities of the rich. This is enough. I am not
upset. And you can't knock his approach – he finished
all the books he began.

White is a great colour   my skin is too rosy to
be white
            pure white of the pillow serving as a rest
for my love's feet at the end of the bed   pure white of the sheets
top sheet rumpled in a heap in the centre   seems like a perfect
backdrop for her long mocha thigh
                              somnolent mocha   cool chocolate
her long thigh
                        lifting together   there is no
telling where that African descent foot will come down   big toe
moving like the heel of a hand at the small of my back   white is a
perfect colour
                cool white pillows plumped behind her shoulder
glass of lemonade beside the bed
evening light outside
                as I get up & walk   white-assed? no, not really,
that's just your imagination, Harold, just your image –
blender to the kitchen to make drinks   hello, moon, hello, open window,
peace to you & all the things you look down upon NAFTA headlines,
daily bread,
            daily cheese, nice shade of dark yellow or would you
call that medium? lime green high heels, these couplings that
in the name of the wind
                        are in your name O moon. Be kind. Go
harvest the young corn &
                        bring my love & I – 4 new potatoes & 2
chicken breasts grilled with mushrooms & polenta.

It was good. I used to enjoy working all day

           & then, after a simple supper of pasta
& artichokes,
    I would stretch out in the bedroom with a big double Haig scotch
in one of those teal blue bottomed glasses you gave me
& listen to a special on Alban Berg from Winnipeg or Montreal,
& Ross Porter's *After Hours* moving towards midnight.
                                 Too much bullshit
& portions of your work get scrambled up. I hadn't listened to very much
    music
for years. But days go by, & weeks, 9 day weeks, Picasso weeks, Matisse
    weeks.

I've had so much financial pressure since last November that my
    stomach's
gone sensitive, no black
                    pepper, no cayenne, even with a few lightly sautéed
shrimps in extra virgin with some parsley tossed on top.
                        Now I'm just not
as amazed by a French horn concerto written shortly after the French
revolution
         or some early work by big-handed Hampton Hawes before he
    went to prison;
plus, my bad luck, I can't enjoy jogging as much as I used to.
What can I say? This isn't Franz Kline time, but it might be time
for the dark blue work pants & the Japanese retreat out in the country
north of Peterborough.

CRAB CAKES W/ BLUEBERRIES

Nobody taught me how to make crab cakes,
it just came to me after eating them a few times in restaurants
like Mortimer's,
                        too fancy, not enough crab, no taste,
or Santa Fe, not far from the Lake.
                                I could have looked them
up in a book like one of Beard's fairly readable volumes;
but instead, I simply went down to the Chinese market
on the east side of Kensington
                        & bought ½ a dozen Atlantic
crabs,
        boiled them in a few tspns of oil, no salt,
& some chopped spring green onions for a few minutes,
& then I took them out to cool.
                        It amazes me that you can
take something like the pale flesh of a crab,
                        Callinectes Sapidus
& make a cake out of it,

                        well, not a cake really, it's more
of a small round patty, but it should be thick,
                                & at least 1½";
the fresh oatmeal & butter was my own idea, I mixed them loose
& then scooped them into patties
                        & sautéed them at a low heat
with some more fresh onions & some chives. I serve them hot

with a dash of mustard & cool blueberries on the side. Any good
beer like a St. Leonard & you've got the restaurant business
beat
        by the distance of a train to Alice Waters in northern
California.

          Florida is blue this morning
its long skinny shape
                like an anatomical part
a part of us
or a part of east Texas, O
                       wow, east Texas is close
& there's some red blur moving across southern Alabama
which may possibly be a political metaphor or just the weather
itself
      & then the Gulf is a wonderful clear shade of darker
blue. Dallas
          is where they shot Kennedy,
blue
      & then smudged with white chalk. White
& then purple grading to vermilion.
We move so easily
it makes flying – say from New York to Portland –
look laborious by comparison. The Carolinas
are calm. We can't see the lush green
of various pastures
              the whole thing is done
almost like a sleight of hand
we concentrate a great deal on the outline
of each state – we are a long way south of Ontario
or Iowa or Massachusetts – how South Carolina
jogs into the Atlantic
not far from that island
where Julie Dash made her film *Daughters of the Dust*
& in the west of North Carolina
we can see the mountains represented by a smudge of rock.

SATORI. I think it's a beautiful word
& I think it means,
                    Loosen up, Let go of some
of your personal biases / each new event is a new event. Ok.

Even some of us who read Basho at 17 or went to see Yojimbo
with friends at a film festival
                              need to do this exercise
over again. Does SATORI mean
                              enlightenment
or does it mean
a letting go of attachment? I can see a touch of Wittgenstein
in this word but as words go it leaves Wittgenstein
breathless. Loosen up,

Reach for the Leica
              or the Hasselblad
& take a photograph. How Zen
& positive observation come together
is amazing

like swimming
or a bush of yellow butterflies exploding into the air.

Perhaps a white bowl of fresh gooseberries
out on the kitchen table after supper with friends.

Their huge & rather graceful grey body
doesn't really move at all

the enormous head tosses once or twice perhaps more
while the eyes fill up with
clear fluid

all the action is in the glands & the tear ducts

When? O I don't know, I think too much dust gets kicked
up by other elephants

Whitman said, When I look at animals they are so peaceful
I could lie down
with them. And I say, yes, yes I understand that poem

perfectly & I'm not sorry that my life is in a state
of ruins

I think I have found something as clear to think about
as Gauss's theory of ordinal numbers

O look out there on the veldt the big guy is coming
toward
me at a distance of about 40 miles hardly moving at all
pausing occasionally to wash the dust
out of his eyes & gorge a few clutches of green leaves.

Peter Tanye comes on at 6 o'clock in the morning
& plays
a Celtic dance by some group from NFLD
& then Custer LaRue who sings with the Baltimore Consort
& then Tanye announces one of Schubert's impromptus –
#2, from the first series, in G minor
played by John O'Connor
who is a fabulous pianist specializing in Schubert & Chopin
that everybody should go out & buy
although Tanye doesn't say so
the CBC is totally noncommercial
that's the word
no hyphen. And so far I've brushed my teeth
& I'm walking around in a loose pale blue shirt
& I've made some coffee. It's overcast
outside
but mild & it's going to be sunny by 10:30. And I think

this is what Canada is it's latitudinal
from NFLD west almost 4200 miles to Vancouver Island
& it should be all blue
with fine red lines dividing the different states
& no Mike Harrises or Brian Mulroneys
just tons of CBC
even though they don't do visual sitcoms
so who needs prat-fall humour – okay, you got one hyphen –
sitcoms is a semi made up word anyway –
And Alexander Mackenzie walked almost all the way across
this enormous latitude

no, uh uh, he didn't get paid or sponsored by Nike
they didn't have Nike in those days or trains or 747s
& Marilyn Bell swam across Lake Ontario
& Vicki Keith swam all 5 lakes both ways
& that's what we're all about, I guess, music & sports
Moscow & Bob Dole don't exist & I head for the shower.

GRAVES

On looking at the pale stone graves
of my Scottish forebears at the Presbyterian
cemetery in the town of Galt:

Hugh Cant's grave   the white-bearded old patriarch
who used to carry a sack of flour on his shoulder
from the mill at Ayr back to Galt once a month,
Duncan Cant
                    Hugh's oldest son & smartest
who lost everything from the New York dental practice
during three frosts in the state of Florida,

Lauren & Howard   the two brothers   both pharmacists,
Hugh's wife   Christie Ferguson   the most beautiful
of the Ferguson girls & the strongest,

Mary Cavers   who married James Warren Donnell
a photographer from Glasgow & produced my father
a son   an only child   raised by crab-apple aunts
a Greek scholar & a good rugby player.

Duncan's first & second wives are buried in New York,
one of his gold pocket watches is buried in Washington
where his first wife Sarah Frances sprang from the Woodwards
& the Ohio Tafts.

None of the Tafts are buried here,
                    but Charles Sabin's wedding picture
dark & serious as the Michigan woods

to the side of me on the wall while I write this
my side
my side of things
the two sides of me going back while the head goes front
Scottish Tao
inward & outward
a way of going
as the Indians went across the lake in their birch canoes.

So surely to God I must know more about birch trees than
my friend James Wong.

We have been here taking up room in southwestern Ontario
for 4 generations now.
Hugh honoured with the flag at half-mast
but everyone else in chaos.
My father spoke as a classicist when he said, "Governments are idiots,"
one succinct sentence,
one brilliant stroke.

I don't know a lot about birch trees.
I know a lot about oranges,
their weight & their colour
each section sweet,
first brought from India to France
in the 15th century
& orange comes from the Indian word *aranga*.

East of Eden
                with its myth of the boy moving
away from the family was written for me.
They gave me a copy for my birthday when I was 11. There
    were
other factors. There were other novels.
There was always a sense of blue infinity
simpler & more marvellous than headmasters at UTS
could have dreamed of slumped
(Philosophers get tired their heads swollen like Grade A eggs)
Protestant & red-faced in western Ontario white pine chairs
unable to define infinity
although we found it easy to live. And by the time I was 20,
or 23½, or 24,
my favourite streets were Gloucester, Dundonald, Isabella.
                                                        The
east of the city. There was always an abundance of chicken pot
pies & good cold beer.
                        There was no gaga social pressure
or rigid white pine chairs in those rundown Victorian
2nd floors I lived in on Church,
cross streets: Dundonald, Gloucester, Isabella,
                                        to do anything
except enjoy myself
                        I was happy. I read a lot
& drank quite a bit but I wasn't comfortable.

        And when I came back
to what people generously refer to

as the liberal arts,
                              Saturday Night
& *Toronto Life*, I was testy. Other people
were variously snotty or generous.

                              I was testy
& sometimes it would affect my body,
                              tension,
muscle spasm,
                    seizure of light
the jellyfish of light rising up in my mind
like a West African beach trophy. "Just cloud patterns,"
a friend of mine said to me, "go with it, & see where
it goes." Okay. I went.

          These days, I want to work all morning
until I'm tired,
                    & then sit in my blue dojo pants
like somebody back from a holiday in Tibet & watch the
          traffic
go past.
          The weather looks good for the next few years.
I miss Church Street
                    (& the way it empties east of Yonge
south through the city & into the Lake) sometimes
                                             but
in a fairly abstract way. Postcards. The things
I love most are like pale green fruit, papayas, sour-sop, pale
          green
mangoes.

          Touch them to my face in the warm Toronto sun, &

                                                    say,
thank you. That was nice. The roast lamb was fantastic. The
rosemary was sweet & bitter & my whole mouth feels fresh
    again.

THE JOGGER

     I like him best in the early morning, he looks good, he's got the whole gear, you know, a slouched outofshape deerstalker, tweed or something like that, tinted goggles, well, you need them, you breathe hard when you jog & he's got really long legs, there are godknows how many different subtle little mineral particles in the Toronto air, he's got a muffler, grey, something like that & a loose windbreaker, it's still cool & the air is fairly damp in March, March is not really a very great month, not at all, loose pants, loose, he would never go in for that black stocking attire, no, not him, never, & Adidas, or Brooks, or whatever, & he runs with slow & patient determination, long legged, taking quite a lot of ground in each stride but not all out, he's not trying to set a track record, & the shoes look comfortable.

ACKNOWLEDGEMENTS

"Olson" & "Crab Cakes w/ Blueberries" first appeared in a very nice little chapbook *Crab Cakes w/ Blueberries* published by Nic Drombolis at Letters Bookstore. "Fabulous Green Beans in a Ten Dollar Wok," "Wynton Marsalis," "Weather Balloons," and "Alex Colville" were first published in *Exile* magazine, winter 2000. "Mangoes" was first published in *China Blues*.

*

Thanks to Peter Buck for his helpful work on "Cogito" and "At The Only Bar," just to mention two; Anita Chong for her cheerful directions; and Paul Vermeersch for his editorial suggestions.

*

My title comes from a classic Leadbelly song called "Goodnight, Irene," where the singer says at one point that sometimes he has a great notion to jump in the goddamn river and drown. I have no such notion, but it's a great title. There are quite a few versions of this song, by various people. Also the Ken Kesey novel. Perhaps this is where he got his title. I was a big fan of Kesey, including *One Flew Over the Cuckoo's Nest*, extraordinarily well-filmed by Milos Forman in the '70s.